Cheerleading
Technique – Training – Show

Miriam Lopez Hernandez de Alba

CHEERLEADING

TECHNIQUE · TRAINING · SHOW

Meyer & Meyer Sport

Orginal title: Cheerleading: Technik – Training – Show
© Meyer & Meyer, 2003
Translated by Heather Ross

British Library Cataloguing in Publication Data
A catalogue record for this book is available from the British Library

Miriam Lopez Hernandez de Alba:
Cheerleading
Technique – Training – Show
Maidenhead: Meyer & Meyer Sport (UK) Ltd, 2004
ISBN: 978-1-84126-273-4

© 2005 by Meyer & Meyer Sport (UK) Ltd.
2nd Edition 2009
Adelaide, Auckland, Budapest, Cape Town, Graz, Indianapolis,
Maidenhead, New York, Olten (CH), Singapore, Toronto
Member of the World
Sport Publishers' Association (WSPA)
Printed and bound by: B.O.S.S Druck und Medien GmbH
ISBN: 978-1-84126-273-4
E-mail: verlag@m-m-sports.com
www.m-m-sports.com

CONTENTS

CHEERLEADING

>> TECHNIQUE · TRAINING · SHOW <<

FOREWORD

Cheerleading has been a feature of sports events in the USA for many years now, and also recently in Europe. Its attractive, enthusiastic and spectacular presentations always make it a great experience for participants and spectators alike.

For the choreography to be correct and for the girls' enthusiasm to really spill over to the crowd, systematic training, concentrated preparation, and competent guidance are necessary.

This is where Miriam Lopez comes in. In this book, she presents her experiences, her knowledge and the results of her work. Her starting point is her many years of practical experience as a dancer and teacher gained in various fields, such as ballet, jazz dance and numerous group fitness courses. Since 2000, she has focused on the supervision of the Cheerleading Group of the Rhein-Fire Düsseldorf football team, a NFL Europe football team, where she has been Head coach since 2002. She is in demand as a consultant in numerous workshops, group camps and even in further education for teachers.

Miriam Lopez's practical experience also includes a solid sports science education, obtained during her lectureship studies at the Institute for Sports Science of the Heinrich-Heine University Düsseldorf from 1998 to 2003. This is where she had the idea of dealing with cheerleading in her thesis. It was a great pleasure to supervise this project and now to see the revised edition published as a monograph – a practical introduction based on the necessary theoretical background.

It just remains for me to wish that this book is read and recognized as widely as it deserves, so that as many potential cheerleaders as possible can benefit from the wealth of knowledge it contains.

Düsseldorf, February 2004

Private Scholar Dr. Theodor Stemper
Fitness and Health Field
Institute for Sports Studies
Heinrich-Heine University Düsseldorf

DEAR READERS,

As General Manager of Rhein Fire, I know how professional this sport is at the highest level. Our 40-strong cheerleader group, the "Pyromaniacs," trains up to five times a week under the guidance of Miriam Lopez, to rehearse new choreography, prepare for the nearly 200 performances it carries out each year and to get fit for shows at our home games in front of 35,000 people.

The overwhelming response from the fans, sponsors and media testifies to the cheerleaders' great success, largely thanks to Miriam Lopez. As an ex-Rhein-Fire cheerleader, she not only possesses the right philosophy and experience, but can also bring the necessary technical know-how that a cheerleading choreographer in the NFL Europe League must have, thanks to her pedagogical dance training and her regular visits to the USA.

When Meyer & Meyer Verlag was looking for a suitable author for this project, it inevitably came across Miriam Lopez, whose many years of successful work with Rhein Fire have made her the most well-known and best cheerleading choreographer in Europe.

Miriam represents everything that matters in modern cheerleading, and that is much more than her feminine charm, her graceful posture and her radiant smile. With her thorough education at the University of Düsseldorf and her professional work ethic, she is the very prototype and role model for every cheerleader.

The formula for success of Miriam Lopez and her girls is a fascinating mixture of good looks, great dancing, regular practice and intelligence.

I wish you great fun in the world of cheerleading.

Alexander Leibkind
General Manager
Rhein Fire Football team Company GmbH

INTRODUCTION

Cheerleading has become a increasingly significant sport over the past few years in Europe. Cheerleaders take part in more and more sports events, TV shows and other public appearances.

There are even events that cannot be imagined without cheerleaders. At first sight, cheerleaders are good-looking young women waving pompoms around and moving to music, but when you look closer and really watch the performance, you soon realize that behind the spectacle there is a serious sport and a lot of hard work. As coach of the Rhein Fire Cheerleaders, I am often asked questions like:

▶ **What is cheerleading?**
▶ **Where can I practice cheerleading?**
▶ **How can I learn cheerleading?**
▶ **What must one watch out for in cheerleading?**
▶ **What makes a good cheerleader?**
▶ **What do cheerleaders need?**

This book answers these and many other questions.

It deals with the subject of cheerleading and contains all the information you need on the subject. Each chapter should be read and understood before cheerleading is offered and taught as a sport. This book is suitable both for beginners and experienced cheerleaders. It is also intended for the increasing number of clubs and schools that would like to offer cheerleading as a sport. There are already many schools that offer cheerleading as a sport in physical education classes. If you look at the sport's development, you can see that it is being taken more and more seriously.

This book looks at the history of cheerleading, starting from the origin of the sport right up to the present day. It describes how to train and gives precise descriptions and explanations of many stretching and strengthening exercises.

The typical technical terms are explained. I set out what you should look out for and what is best avoided. Jumps and jump drills are described, and drills and pointers are also given on the subjects of dance, cheers, chants and stunts. Precise explanations are given as to what cheerleading is all about and which rules are generally accepted, especially concerning behavior and public appearances. I give advice on learning these rules and on what makes a good cheerleader.

The book presents the basics of learning for potential cheerleaders and the basics of teaching for coaches and teachers.

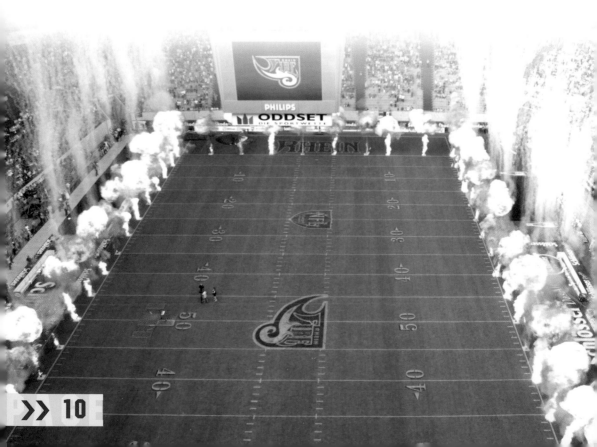

1 THE HISTORY OF CHEERLEADING

1.1 ITS DEVELOPMENT IN THE USA

Careful study reveals that cheerleading was already practiced in ancient Greece, where the crowds encouraged and supported their sporting heroes in the Olympic Games with cheerleaders. Perhaps this motivated the athletes to achieve good results.

Cheering and encouragement from the spectators in the stands form the foundation of cheerleading as we know it today.

America, the motherland of cheerleading, can look back on a 100-year history of cheerleading, which began at a college in Minnesota.

In the 19th century, nearly all college students were men, and they naturally tended to watch the sporting events held at their High Schools.

In 1898, the University of Minnesota football team was having a pretty bad season, losing nearly every match. The students met up and discussed how best to support and motivate their team. Up to this time, the students cheered the players from the stands and wanted to help them. But the cheering was very disorganized and fizzled out. Often the players couldn't hear the students' message at all as the spectators' shouts were not coordinated.

It was decided to organize the cheering and one student, Johnny Campbell, took on this task. He was the first cheerleader and became the forerunner of the movement.

On November 2, the University of Minnesota football team played badly once again. Campbell stood up from his seat in the auditorium, stood in front of the crowd and organized the cheering. He shouted various *cheers*, which everyone then repeated, shouting together. The team was inspired with this support and won the game, and the success was attributed to the cheering of the spectators led by Campbell. From that day on, a few men always stood on the edge of the field and organized the cheering.

Cheers such as "RAH, RAH, RAH! SKU-U-MAH, HOO-RAH! HOO-RAH! VARSITY! MINN-E-SO-TAH!" were among the first and were very popular.

And so a new movement was born in the USA. But then, the cheerleaders were all men. Women did not get involved until the 20th century, when the first megaphone was also used. It made it easier for the spectators to recognize and take up the battle cries. With the entry of women, the nature of cheerleading changed. Gymnastics, dance and even acrobatic elements were incorporated into the program, and cheerleading was introduced into high schools.

In 1927, the first training book for cheerleaders was published under the title "Just Yell."

In the 1930s, the first pompoms appeared. They were brightly colored and, at that time, were still made out of wool or paper. They were used to make the cheerleaders' movements stand out more.

In the 1940s, many Americans were drafted into World War II. This changed the structure of the teams, as almost 90% of the team members were now female.

A great wave of enthusiasm swept the country, and cheerleading was offered and practiced everywhere.

In 1948, Laurence Herkinger, after whom a jump, the "Herkie", would later be named, organized the first cheerleader camp and founded the first cheerleader organization, the NCA (National Cheerleading Association). The camp was held in Huntsville at the University and 52 participants attended. In the second year, there were 350 participants and, a few years later, around 20,000 cheerleaders attended his camps. Herkinger has done a great deal to popularize this sport.

During the '50s, cheerleading spread widely, and professional football teams formed cheerleader groups.

Since 1978, the annual Cheerleading Championships has taken place in the USA. Judges were trained and ever since, a selected jury has chosen the best team in the country at the championships. In 1986, the height of a pyramid or stunt was laid down in the rules.

These events in the USA were televised, and cheerleading became increasingly popular and cheerleading teams came in the public eye more and more. Sporting events became unthinkable without them.

In 1996, it was estimated that more than 600,000 cheerleaders were active on different teams in the USA.

2 WARM-UP

2.1   GENERAL PREPARATIONS

The warm-up is a very important part of practice. Every practice session should start with a short warm-up in order to prepare the body for the work to come.

The importance of the warm-up is often underestimated, which is a great mistake.

The warm-up not only prepares the body for the exercise to follow, it also improves general motivation, coordination and mental readiness to perform.

The warm-up consists of four main functions:

1. **Warming-up**
2. **Preparation**
3. **Preventing injury**
4. **Building team spirit**

The warm-up involves moving the whole body, as well as individual joints.

The whole-body movement raises the body temperature and stimulates metabolism. Certain nerve impulses are faster at a higher body temperature, and the activity of the motor systems in the brain increases, thereby increasing coordination ability, attention and reactivity. The danger of injury is considerably reduced.

The joints usually need more time to be prepared for movement, which is why the warm-up includes movements that isolate specific joints, e.g. shoulder circles.

The warm-up also stimulates the cardiovascular system and speeds up the blood flow to the muscles, thereby creating the conditions for higher oxygen uptake.

Suitable warm-up activities are a 5 to 10-minute aerobic program with such movements as the Box Step, Jumping Jack, V-Step, Step Touch, etc.

It is important that the cheerleading warm-up include a stretching program that is repeated in every warm-up.

Stretching is an important part of cheerleading, as many dances, jumps, cheers and chants include elements requiring a great deal of flexibility. A high kick, for example, should never be performed without stretching the legs beforehand, to be precise the muscles at the back of the leg (**see photo**). The danger of pulling a muscle is very high without stretching, and not only for high kicks. To be a good cheerleader, you must be able to do splits, and to learn this, you must stretch very frequently and very intensively.

You should not expect to be able to do everything perfectly after just one practice session, though. The body must get used to the new movements, and you must be disciplined and train at least two or three times a week, before being successful.

The structure of a warm-up can vary, but the important thing is that the group has fun recognizes the value of the warm-up. Varying music and methods, for example stretching, ensures that the warm-up always offers a new challenge and is never boring.

2.2   STRETCHING METHODS

Over time, the following two stretching techniques have prevailed:

1. Active stretching
2. Passive stretching

Active stretching is a self-directed stretch, i.e. a muscle is stretched because its antagonist is working. **Passive stretching** is an other-directed stretch, i.e. it requires an external influence, e.g. a partner, piece of equipment, etc. Both techniques can be further divided into **static** and **dynamic stretching**.

▶Active-Dynamic Stretching

A stretch position is adopted, the agonist of the muscle to be stretched is tensed and the tension is maintained for 5-7 seconds. The stretch position is then held for another 10-20 seconds. The tension is then slowly released.

▶Active-Dynamic Stretching

Adopt a stretch position, but this time, swing gently in this position. Swing rhythmically and only up to the pain threshold to increase the amplitude of the movement of the joint.

▶Passive-Static Stretching

This is often called the "real" stretching technique, or **stretching**. The muscle is stretched slowly; no pain should be felt. The position should be held for 10-30 seconds. The degree of stretch is correct if the feeling of tension decreases during this time.

▶Passive-Dynamic Stretching

A partner brings the cheerleader to the limit of movement by rhythmic stretching, and holds the stretch at that point for about 15 seconds.

Basically, you should stick to the following points when stretching:

> ▶ Always stretch calmly and gently
> ▶ Always concentrate on the muscle being stretched
> ▶ Always breathe regularly and calmly, increase the stretch when exhaling
> ▶ Stretching should never be painful
> ▶ The practice area temperature should be comfortable

2.3   STRETCHING EXERCISES

▶ Neck Muscle Stretch

This exercise mainly stretches the lateral neck muscles, the deltoid (m. deltoideus) and trapezius muscles (m. trapezius).

The right hand grips the head over the left ear. The head leans to the right and pulling the left arm and the left shoulder downward increases the stretching effect. The back is kept straight and the legs are slightly bent, the knees and the toes point outward.

Perform the exercise on both sides of the body.

▶ Shoulder and Arm Muscle Stretch I

This exercise mainly stretches the triceps (m. triceps brachii), the pectoral muscle (m. pectoralis, the lat muscles (m. latissiums dorsi) and part of the shoulder muscles.

The right hand grips the left elbow and brings the left arm behind the head so that the left hand touches the back between the shoulder blades. Now press the elbow down carefully with the right hand toward the back. Keep the back straight during this exercise. The knees are slightly bent and they and the toes point outwards.

Perform this exercise on the right and the left sides of the body.

▶ Shoulder and Arm Muscle Stretch II

This exercise mainly stretches the deltoid muscle (m. deltoideus), the trapezius (m. trapezius), the rhomboid muscles (m. rhomboideus) and the triceps muscle (m. triceps brachii).

This exercise is performed from a standing position, the knees are slightly bent and they and the toes point outward. Grip the top of the left arm with the right hand and push it to the left at shoulder height in front of the body. Increase the stretching effect by holding the left elbow and pushing it behind the back. The upper body remains upright.

Perform this exercise on both sides of the body.

▶ Shoulder and Arm Muscle Stretch III

This exercise mainly stretches the wrist flexor (m. flexor carpi ulnaris) and the finger flexors (m. flexor digitorum).

In a standing position, the left hand grips the right hand from inside. The right arm is extended and the fingers of the right hand point toward the body, thus forming a stretch.

Carry out with the left and right hands.

▶ **Shoulder and Arm Muscle Stretch IV**
This exercise mainly stretches the wrist extensors (m. extensor carpi ulnaris) and the finger extensors (m. extensor digitorum).

In the standing position, the left hand grips the fingers of the right hand and pulls them toward the body, while the right arm is extended.

Carry out with the left and right hands.

▶ **Lateral Torso Muscle Stretch**
This exercise primarily stretches the lat muscles (m. latissimus dorsi), the external, oblique abdominals (m. obliquus externus abdominis) and the square lumbar muscle (m. quadratus lumborum).

Bring the left arm over the head to the right and at the same time, bring the right arm to the left in front of the hips. The upper body also leans to the right. The knees are slightly bent and relaxed, and the knees and toes point outwards. The body weight is distributed evenly over both legs.

Also perform this exercise to the left side.

The previous exercises also stretch the lateral torso muscles, while also stretching the adductors and the rear thigh muscles.

Stand with your feet apart and legs straight. The back is also straight and at a 90° angle to the floor. Stretch your left arm over to the right, with your head in line with your spine and look at the floor.

From the above position, bring your upper body toward your right leg. Try to bring your head down as far as it will go, but without placing it on your knee and keep your back straight.

Perform these exercises on the other side of the body also.

This exercise stretches the right and left side of the body at the same time. The aim is to bend the upper body down as low as possible.

▶ **Rear Thigh Muscle Stretch**

This exercise mainly stretches the rear thigh muscles (Mm. Ischiocrurales).

From a standing position, stretch the right leg out to the front. Place the heel on the ground and flex the right foot so that the toes point upward. The left leg is bent. Both knees are at the same height and are placed together. The upper body leans forward; keeping the back flat, until you can feel a stretch behind the right thigh. Support yourself by placing your hands on your left knee. Increase the stretch by leaning further forward. Always make sure that the back remains flat.

Perform the same exercise with the left leg.

▶ **Adductor Stretch**

This exercise stretches mainly the adductors.

Sit in the straddle position and lean the upper body forward, keeping the back flat. The knees point upward and both the knees and feet are extended. The important thing is not how far forward your upper body can lean, but keeping the back flat and stopping the stretch before it starts to hurt.

▶ Stretch Variations

This exercise stretches the adductors and the lateral torso muscles.

The upper body leans to the right while you sit in a straddle position. As you exhale, try to bring the upper body down toward the right leg. It is important to hold the left arm above the head and keep it there so as not to tip over and stretch the "wrong" muscles.

Also perform this exercise on the left side.

This exercise stretches the rear thigh muscles and back muscles.

Sit in the straddle position and bend the upper body over the left leg, keeping the back flat and the shoulders parallel. Drape the front of the body over the leg.

Also perform this exercise on the right side.

▶ **Adductor Stretch with Sideways Lunge**

This exercise stretches the adductors.

Starting from the standing straddle position, transfer your weight over the right leg. Place the hands on the bent right knee. The left leg must be straight. The stretch should be felt in the left leg. Press the left hand on the left knee to intensify the stretch.

▶ **Adductor Stretch with Ankle Mobilization**

This exercise also stretches the adductors.

From a squatting position, transfer your weight to the right leg. Extend the left leg forward and point the left foot. After a few seconds, flex the foot so that the toes point upward.

Repeat this action a few times, not only to stretch the adductors, but also to mobilize the ankle joint.

Perform this exercise on the other side of the body.

▶ Rear Thigh Muscle Stretch

This exercise mainly stretches the rear thigh muscles and the lumbar spine muscles.

Place the feet together and go into a squatting position. Grip the heels and "un-roll" the upper body slowly upward. Keep holding the heels and straighten the legs. Keep the head and the shoulders relaxed. Then slowly straighten the upper body. It helps to concentrate on straightening one vertebra at a time. Finally, straighten the head. It is important that the legs are completely straight before starting to unroll the upper body.

▶ General Leg Stretch

These exercises stretch the rectus femoris, the m. illiopsoas, the m. gluteus maximus and the mm. ischiocrurales.

In a forward lunge, the rear knee is brought as far backward as possible. Keeping the upper body upright, try to push the hips toward the floor. Transfer your body weight forward to stretch all of the above muscles.

Also perform on the other side of the body.

Starting from a lunge position, straighten the back leg, creating a 90° angle at the right knee. The knee should not extend beyond the toe. The upper body is upright and the body weight lies over the front leg.

During this exercise, bring the arms out to the sides without changing the leg position. This develops the balance and also strengthens the participating muscles.

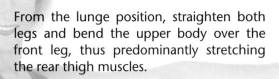

From the lunge position, straighten both legs and bend the upper body over the front leg, thus predominantly stretching the rear thigh muscles.

Carry out on both sides of the body.

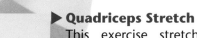

▶ Quadriceps Stretch

This exercise stretches the quadriceps muscles.

Stand with both feet together, then hold the right foot with the right hand and bend the leg so that the right foot touches the bottom. Keep the knees together, the left leg straight and the upper body upright. You can stretch the left arm out to the front to keep your balance.

▶ **Calf Stretch**

This exercise stretches the soleus (m. triceps surae) and the gastrocnemius (m. gastrocnemius) muscles.

Bend the right leg and extend the left leg backward. It is important that the rear foot is flat on the floor. Create a stretch in the calf muscles by making sure the hips face forward and deliberately pressing the rear foot into the ground. The upper body is upright.

Pulling the arms upward intensifies the stretch.

Also perform this exercise on the other side of the body.

Every stretch should be held for between 10-30 seconds. These exercises require passive-static stretching.

2.4   STRENGTH TRAINING/EXERCISES

Strength training is another important training component:

It is particularly important for a cheerleader to have a good, sporty figure. As most cheerleader costumes show a bare midriff, it doesn't look good if the stomach, legs or arms are not toned and in shape.

The following exercises help to tone the body and burn unwanted fat:

▶ **Abdominal Strengthening I**
This exercise mainly strengthens the upper abdominal muscles (m. rectus abdominus).

The arms are placed on the floor behind the head, taking care that the elbows point outward. The legs are bent and shoulder-width apart on the floor. The abdominal muscles are tensed so that the lumbar spine touches the floor. Abdominal and bottom muscles are tensed to avoid the participation of the hip flexors.

In the exhalation phase, lift the shoulder blades off the floor, but keep the lower back on the floor. Do not bring the face toward the knees, look at the ceiling and lift the shoulders upward too.

▶ **Abdominal Strengthening II**
This exercise mainly strengthens the external oblique abdominal muscle (m. obliquus externus abdominis).

Lie on your back, with your lumbar spine touching the floor throughout the exercise. Stretch the left arm out to the side at shoulder height and place the right hand behind the head. Bend the right arm. As you exhale, lift the right shoulder by raising the upper body from the floor and moving it to the left. Lay the left foot on the right knee.

Also perform this exercise on the right side.

▶ **Abdominal Strengthening III**
This exercise mainly strengthens the lower rectus abdominis and the triceps muscle of the upper arm.

Lie on your back and bend the knee and hip joints, with the feet pointing at the floor. At the same time, lay the arms beside the body on the floor. Then raise the hips just by tensing the abdominal muscles, and pushing the arms against the floor.

Work by using muscle strength, not by bouncing. This exercise requires well-developed abdominal muscles. Make sure you breathe evenly.

▶ **Strengthening the Torso**

This exercise mainly strengthens the back extensor muscles (m. iliocostalis), the bottom muscles and the shoulder muscles.

Lie on your stomach and lift your left arm and right leg from the floor. The hips should not lose contact with the floor. The chin is supported by the right hand.

Before performing this exercise, you must be able to maintain a certain basic tension in the back, abdominal and bottom muscles.

Then carry out the exercise on the other side of the body.

▶ **Arm, Shoulder and Chest Strengthening**

This exercise mainly strengthens the triceps and biceps muscles of the upper arm, the trapezius muscle, the deltoid and the pectorals.

Modified push-up position:

The abdominal and back muscles are tensed and the arms are about shoulder-width apart. The body should form a straight line from the knees to the head. Lower the body to the floor by bending the arms and raise it again by straightening the arms. Keep the head in line with the spine.

Push-up position:

The body is now in a straight line from the feet to the head. Keep the hips in the correct position and don't hollow your back. Position your shoulders above your hands. Bend the arms to lower the body and straighten them to raise it again.

▶ Leg Strengthening I

This exercise mainly strengthens the abductor, adductor and lateral abdominal muscles.

Lie on your side, supported on your bent arm with the elbow on the floor. Keep the body in a straight line and maintain basic tension. Now raise the top leg and hold this position for a few seconds, then lower the leg again.

Carry out this exercise on both sides of the body.

▶ Leg Strengthening II

This exercise mainly strengthens the abductor, the gluteus medius and the tensor fasciae latae muscles.

Sit on the floor with the hands resting on the right knee and the left leg stretched out to the side. The upper body is upright. Raise the straight leg and keep the foot pointed.

Then, bend the raised leg and continue the exercise with the leg bent.

These exercises should also be performed on the other side of the body.

▶ **Leg Strengthening III**

This exercise mainly strengthens the quadriceps, formed by the rectus femoris, the vastus medialis, lateralis and intermedius.

Bend both legs slightly in a lunge position. The rear knee should be bent so that it almost touches the floor. The right knee is at a 90° angle to the floor. Extend the arms out to the front to help keep balance. The upper body is upright.

Carry out this exercise on both sides of the body.

▶ Bottom and Leg Strengthening I

This exercise mainly strengthens the bottom (gluteus maximus), rear thigh and back extensor muscles.

From a kneeling position, raise one leg in the air. Keep the back flat and do not let it hollow. Always make sure that the pelvis is stabilized by keeping the stomach muscles tense. Now make small upward movements with the upper leg. Work by using muscle strength and not by swinging. Do not let the head sink into the neck during this exercise.

Carry out the exercise with left and right leg.

▶ Bottom and Leg Strengthening II

This exercise strengthens the same muscles as the previous exercise.

From a kneeling position, raise one leg to the side, until the knee and foot of the raised leg are the same height. Then, take the leg backward and extend it upward. Lastly, bring the leg back to the side.

Carry out this exercise with right and left legs.

▶ Calf Muscle Strengthening

This exercise mainly strengthens the calf muscle (m. triceps surae).

Reach a stable standing position and bend one leg. After tensing the abdominal muscles, raise the heel of the support leg so the body weight is on the ball of the foot and lower it again. Repeat this movement a few times and then change the support leg and do the same thing on the other leg.

Repeat each exercise 10 or 15 times, then rest for a few seconds and then perform the exercise another 10-15 times. Then move on to the next exercise. (The number of repetitions can be increased gradually.)

3 MOTIONS

3.1 MOTION QUALITY (ARM MOVEMENTS)

The motions are among the most important components of cheerleading, and in cheerleading, they mainly refer to arm movements.

Although there are countless different teams, all cultivating their own styles, the clarity and precision of the motions have enabled the motions to be adopted by all of them. All cheerleaders use the same basic motions and follow the same rules.

Motions are arm movements that must be performed with a certain power. Synchronization is important within the team, as it is a sign of quality. Also, the spectators at the top of the stands in a full stadium also want to see the cheerleaders' movements performed cleanly (c.f. photo). Tight, fast and snappy movements that are synchronized are easier for the spectators to make out than light, flowing motions.

This is why we talk about the **sharpness** of motions. Motions must be performed sharply and precisely. By sharpness, we mean firmness and abruptness of execution.

Frequent, intensive practice is required to master the motions. Every motion is precisely defined and should not deviate from the definition if possible.

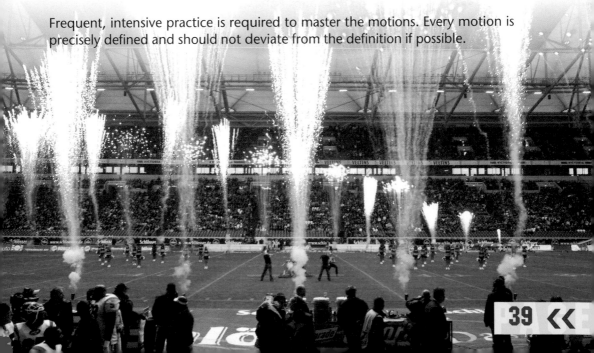

Motions form the basis of many important cheerleading movement patterns. Cheers and chants consist almost entirely of sequences of motions, but motions are also important in dances and pyramids, which will be addressed in later chapters.

In championships, motions form one of the most important judging criteria.

Motions are best practiced in front of a mirror, as the cheerleader can then see for herself immediately if her arms are in the right position or not.

The coach demonstrates the arm action and explains how to perform it.

The group must then imitate the motion, remembering what the coach has just said.

Make sure that all motions are carried out so that you can always see your arms. Even when the arms are stretched out to the sides, they shouldn't be taken so far backward that you can't see them any more. One criterion for good motions is that you must be able to see your arms without moving your head.

Once you have learned the execution of the motions and acquired an understanding of the concepts, you can practice the motions as follows:

The coach stands in front of the group and shouts the name of a certain motion, e.g. "High V." The group tries to perform the correct motion as fast as possible. Practice all motions in this way, until the motions and their respective names have been learned by heart. After a few run-throughs, increase the speed so that the motions are performed in rapid succession one after the other. This exercise can also be used in the warm-up, with the difference that the group runs in place while the coach shouts the names of the motions.

To test whether the motions are performed sharply enough, the cheerleaders form pairs. One cheerleader performs a motions and her partner tries to modify them. For example, the partner can try to shake the other girl's arms. If her motions cannot be easily changed and the movement resists the pressure of the partner, then they are performed with enough tightness and power. The cheerleader has learned where her arms should be.

The most important hand and arm motions are listed below.

3.2   HAND MOTIONS

▶ **Bucket**

This motion is so-called because the hand makes a fist as if it is gripping a bucket handle. The thumb wraps around the fingers and the back of the hand faces upward. The fist forms an extension of the arm; do not let your wrist bend.

▶ **Candle Sticks**

In this motion, the inside of the hand is turned forward. Simply adopt the **Bucket** motion and then make a quarter turn so that the fingers point in the direction of the crowd. This motion looks as if you are holding a candlestick in your hand, hence the name **Candle Stick**.

▶ **Blades**

In this motion, the hand is as flat as possible, with the fingers held together. The hand forms an extension of the arm. Do not let your wrist bend.

3.3   ARM MOTIONS

▶ **High V**

The arms are stretched above the head in a V shape. Make sure that the hands are turned so that the palms of the hands face outward. The thumbs are wrapped inside the fists and point away from the body, i.e. outward. The arms must be locked and form a straight line with the hands. Make sure that the wrist does not bend.

Do not raise the shoulders when you perform the motions.

▶ **Low V**

This motion is the opposite of the High V. In the Low V, the arms stretch downward to form an upside-down V. Make sure that the palms of the hands face into the body and the backs of the hands face outward. The hands form fists and the thumbs wrap around the other fingers, so that the thumbs also face into the body. The arms are locked and the wrists must not bend.

▶ T-Motion

Here, the arms are stretched out to the sides, and it is very important that the elbows are straight and do not sag. The hands form a fist and the palms of the hands face downward to the floor. The arms are exactly shoulder height, and the arms and body form a T shape.

▶ Half-T

This is a modification of the T-Motion. The arms are still at shoulder height, but in this motion, they are bent at the elbows instead of being fully extended to the sides. The elbows point outward, and the fists are in front of the shoulders in the Bucket Position.

The shoulders must not be raised.

▶ Touchdown

This motion is so-called, because the football referee performs the same action after a touchdown. If one team manages to bring or throw the football into the opposite end zone (the ball must then be caught), they get six points, or a touchdown.

The cheerleader touchdown motion is, unlike that of the referee, performed with locked arms. Extend the arms above the head, with the upper arms almost touching the ears. The hands can form a fist or a blade, the important thing is that the palms of the hands face each other. The arms must not be placed too far behind the head. As in all other motions, your hands should still be in your range of vision, and you should not raise your shoulders.

▶ Low Touchdown

This motion is the opposite of the Touchdown. Extend the arms downward in front of your body, keeping them parallel to each other and forming a straight line from the shoulders to the fingertips. The palms of the hands should face each other.

▶ Right Diagonal

The diagonals are difficult to learn, as to perform them perfectly you need good body awareness and coordination.

In this motion, the right arm hits a High V and the left arm a Low V. Ideally, the arms should form a straight line from the right fist to the left fist.

▶ Left Diagonal

In this motion, everything is the same in principle as in the Right Diagonal, except that in this motion the left arm hits a High V and the right arm hits a Low V.

If the diagonal runs from top left to bottom right, it is called a Left Diagonal, if it runs from top right to bottom left, it is called a Right Diagonal.

▶ Right L

In this motion, the arms form an L-shape. In a Right L, the right arm is in the Touchdown position and the left arm is in the T position. Both arms must be kept straight.

▶ Left L

The Left L is the opposite motion to the Right L motion, so that the left arm is in the Touchdown position and the right arm is in the T position.

▶ Arms on the Table

In this motion, the position of the arms looks like the name.

The arms are bent at 90°. Make sure that the arms are parallel to each other; they are held in front of the body so that the upper arms also form a 90° angle with the body. (In this position, you could easily put your arms on the table.)

▶ Punch

The right arm hits the Touchdown position close to the right ear and the left hand is placed on the left hip. The left hand forms a fist and the back of the hand faces forward.

▶ Right K

Here, the body forms a shape that looks like a K. The right arm is in the High V position and the left arm crosses at a 45° angle in front of the upper body, so that the right hand is pointing at the floor. The left arm is also locked.

The legs are in the lunge position. The right leg is bent, and the left leg is straight.

▶ Left K

The opposite of the Right K is the Left K, i.e., the same movement is performed but in the opposite direction. Now, the left arm hits the High V position and the right arm crosses in front of the upper body. The legs form a lunge to the other side, i.e., the left leg is now bent and the right leg is straight.

▶ Arms on Hips

The hands form fists and are placed on the hips, making sure that the elbows point out to the sides. Pull the shoulders back to ensure an upright posture, which is very important in the performance of the motions.

▶ Variation

One variation is to place the hands further back on the hips.

Here, the flat hands are placed on either side of the back so that the fingertips point to the floor.

▶ Daggers

There are various different ways to perform the Dagger Motion, but in all of them, you should make sure that the elbows point into the waist and the fists point upward. The fists can either be directly in front of the shoulders or, as in our photo, point out to the side. It is important also that the palms of the hands face inward.

Incorrect Arm Position

The arms should never be held like this. The wrist should not bend upward or downward in the motions.

In addition to these hand and arm motions, there are also two more clapping variations.

3.4 CLAPS

▶1. Clap

The hands are held in the blade position and pressed together. The fingers are together and the hands are flat. The elbows are held close to the body.

▶2. Clasp

The hands clasp each other when they touch. The elbows are kept close to the body.

3.5 LEG MOTIONS

There are a few leg motions that are characteristic features of cheerleading.

Briefly, they are as follows:

▶ **Right Lunge**
The right leg is bent and the left leg is straight. Make sure that the right knee does not extend beyond the level of the toes; if possible, it should be above the heel. The toes and the knee point outward, thus turning the whole leg outward. The upper body should be upright.

▶ **Left Lunge**
The left leg is bent and the right leg is straight. In the Left Lunge, too, make sure that the foot and knee face outward. It is the opposite of the Right Lunge.
Side Liberty Hitch

▶ The left leg is straight and the right leg is bent. The right foot is exactly at the same height as the left knee. Make sure that the inside of the right foot touches the side of the left knee. The knee faces forward and the raised foot must be pointed.

You can combine the motions together, thus giving new variations.

Here are a few examples:

4 CHANTS

4.1 TIPS FOR LEARNING CHANTS

A chant is a combination of words and actions. It is a kind of speech-song consisting of very few words, used for encouragement. Unlike cheers, chants can be shouted spontaneously throughout the game. Various chants are required to animate the crowd during the various different game situations. The crowd is supposed to shout the chants along with the cheerleaders, to support the team. The cheer team shouts the chant once by themselves and the second time, the crowd ought to join in.

It is important to have a large repertoire of chants so that the performance does not get boring. If you always perform the same chants, no matter how well they are performed, after a while, the crowd will get bored. The chant can look different every time with small changes in the movements or in the order, even though it is not new.

A chant must be mastered by the whole group, for it is not uncommon to change position during a chant, and you must then concentrate on several things at once. The chant must become automatic, so that other tasks can be performed at the same time.

To learn a chant, you should first master the short text and above all get the accentuation right. It is also the best idea to repeat the text a few times, without the motions. When you are sure of the words and the accentuation, then you can add the motions. Ideally, you should learn the chants in front of a mirror then you can check immediately if you are in time with the other cheerleaders. Chants are particularly good for changing position or when forming a pyramid.

A chant can be repeated as often as you wish; the only important thing is that the team stops at the same time. The captain shouts the command "Last Time" during the chants, so that she and the team know that this will be the last repetition of the chant.

The captain is the cheerleader chosen by the coach, who decides which cheer, chant or Eight Count should be performed during the game. So she acts as the right hand of the coach and should be respected by the rest of the team.

During the chant, it is important that the voices are loud and clear. It is also a good opportunity to build up eye contact with the crowd.

4.2   CHANTS TO LEARN TOGETHER

▶ **1. Defense Go!**
DEFENSE
Take one step to the right with the right leg, then slap your thighs twice, shouting "DE-FENSE."

Lean forward slightly.

GO
On the word "Go," bring the left leg in and the feet together and the arms perform the motions shown. After the word "Go" there is a short pause.

This chant is now performed in the other direction, i.e., starting with the left foot.

▶**2. Go, Fight, Win!**

GO

On the word "Go," perform the K motion to the left, with the head facing forward.

FIGHT

On the word "Fight," bring the right leg in and hit a High V with the arms.

WIN

On the word "Win," bring the arms down from a High V to a Low V. Make a lunge forward onto the left foot. Bend both knees and distribute your body weight evenly over both legs.

Clasp

After the word "Win," pull the right foot back and place both feet together.

Clasp the hands and then pause briefly. After the clasp, repeat the chant once more.

▶ **3. FIRE GO!**

FI-

Step forward onto the right foot, straighten the legs and push the hips forward. The first row stops on the syllable "Fi" with the arms in a Low V, and the second row stops with the arms in a High V.

-RE

On the syllable "Re," both rows cross their arms in front of the chest. The legs are in the same position as before, but the hips are now tilted backward.

GO
On the word "GO," the first row hits a High V and the second row a Low V. The hips are pushed forward again.

Clasp
The legs do not move during this *Chant*. On the word "Go," both rows take the arms in front of the chest and do a *Clasp*, because at this point, there should be a short break. The hips are tilted backward again during the *Clasp*. Repeat the *Chant* after the break.

5 CHEERS

5.1 INTRODUCTION AND USAGE

Cheers also consist of a combination of words and movements. They are much longer than chants and are not repeated. A cheer always consists of several lines, most of which rhyme. A cheer is not only longer than a chant but also has a completely different purpose. They always tell a short, appropriate story and cannot just be inserted during the ongoing game, unlike the chant. A cheer is only performed during the official time-outs or before and after a game, i.e., during a pause. This should always be observed, for during a cheer, the cheer team wants to ensure that they have the crowd's full attention during the cheer. This can only happen during a break.

A cheer should always have a positive message to motivate the crowd and the team.

A cheer always has an appropriate beginning and an appropriate ending. Cheers can differ greatly. They are as different as the teams themselves. Many cheers are dance-based and others are more gymnastic; the content and effect are up to the cheer team, there is no right or wrong style.

To learn a cheer, you should first learn the text, just as you did with the chants.

You can learn them by reading through the text a few times and then get the accentuation right. The accentuation is crucial in a cheer, as it determines when the movements take place: a movement always takes place on an accentuated syllable. It is not necessary and often not even possible to perform a movement for each word.

Once you have learned the text and the accentuation, look at yourself for the first three or four movements. Try to perform them fitting them in with the text. Repeat a few times until you feel more confident. Only then will you be ready to deal with the next movements. Then learn the new movements with the corresponding text, separately from the old movements, and then perform the first one immediately followed by the new one. Continue like this until you have learned the whole cheer. It is important to watch yourself while you are learning a cheer. A mirror is very useful, but another person watching you is also helpful. This person should be prepared to correct you for it is only through correction that a team can achieve perfection.

The voice is also very important. You should try to "pull" the voice from the stomach. Make sure that you don't shriek.

When you have mastered this, you should then work on your personality, as this is just as important as tightly executed motions. You should always have a smile on your face and look at the crowd. Eye contact gets spectators involved.

You can also incorporate jumps into a cheer.

"COME ON TEAM!"

"YELL IT LOUD!"

"WIN THAT GAME!"

"WE WANT MORE!"

"SPIRIT SCORE!"

"LET'S BE PROUD!"

5.2 EXAMPLES

▶ 1. COME ON TEAM

COME ON

Step forward onto the right foot, keeping the back straight and leaning forward. The outstretched arms are crossed in front of the body, the knees are bent.

TEAM

The left leg is pulled into the pose, the left foot is next to the right knee so that the left knee points forward. The right arm hits the Touchdown motion and the left hand is placed on the left hip. The left elbow points backward.

▶ **2. YELL IT LOUD**

YELL IT

Step forward onto the left foot, both legs are straight. The arms hit the T motion, the upper body is upright.

LOUD

The right leg is straightened and brought next to the straight left leg, and the arms are brought toward the body.

▶ **3. SPIRIT SCORE**

SPIRIT

The first row makes a lunge with the left leg to the left. The right leg remains straight. The right arm is extended to the left in front of the body at shoulder height and the left hand is placed on the hip. The second row waits.

SCORE

The second row performs the above movement on the word "Score." The first row stays in the same position as before.

▶ **4. WE WANT MORE**

WE WANT

The right leg is extended behind the left leg, preparing for a pencil turn. The arms are brought down straight by the side close to the body. Stand on the balls of the feet.

No words are spoken as you spin around to the right.

MORE

After the turn, bring the arms up into the High V position and stand on the tips of the toes. The whole body is extended.

▶ 5. WIN THAT GAME

WIN
Step forward onto the right foot, while you bring the right arm down from the High V position straight against the body, touching the thigh.

THAT
On the word "That," bring the left arm down straight against the body.

GAME
The left leg is brought next to the right leg and the hands form a clasp.

▶ **6. LET'S BE PROUD**

LET'S BE

Make a lunge forward onto the right leg, so that you are kneeling on one knee, while crossing the arms in front of the body, and bending the head toward the floor.

PROUD

The arms are stretched up into the High V position. The upper body is straight and the head is raised. The tip of the right foot touches the ground.

6 JUMPS

6.1 PRELIMINARY REMARKS

Jumps constitute a major element of cheerleading. The role of the cheer team is always to entertain the crowd and to provide a good show. A well-executed jump is particularly eye-catching, and a successful, well-synchronized jump is a real crowd-pleaser. Jumps are not easy to learn and to really master a jump requires long and hard practice. Do not perform a jump in public until it is perfect. Jumps can be performed in various situations, which is one reason for the popularity of jumps with cheerleaders and spectators alike. You can include jumps either before or after a cheer or dance. Jumps often take place at the start of a game, e.g., when the players run onto the field. It really doesn't matter when a jump takes place; the only important thing is not to jump in negative situations, e.g., when the team has lost. A jump is always a sign of joy. It is often used with the team has had a successful performance, as an expression of pride and celebration.

You must think of several things at the same time in a jump. Arms, legs, position of the upper body, the head, the landing and timing are all important factors in a jump. They must all be in the right position at the same time and no factor can be forgotten or neglected.

6.2 JUMP PHASES

Every jump can be divided into four phases, and the cheerleader must master all four.

1. Preparation

2. Lift

3. Execution

4. Landing

▶ 1. Preparation

The height of the jump is very important. The cheerleader should try to jump as high as possible, to give her a long flight. The longer the cheerleader remains in the air, the more time she has to perform the jump correctly.

Preperation provides momentum for the jump in which the arms, legs and feet play an important part.

In the starting position, the feet are together and the arms are by the side of the body. On a certain signal, e.g., in the music or on a certain word, the cheerleader reacts and starts to prepare for the jump. Place the arms in the High V position and go onto the tips of the toes. In the next step, bring the arms down from the High V and cross them in front of the body, to increase impetus in the take-off. While the arms are crossed, bend the knees slightly and shift your body weight onto the tips of your toes.

The preperation should be carried out simultaneously by the whole squad, to ensure a synchronized jump.

▶ 2. Lift

In a successful lift, the cheerleader pushes firmly off the ground from the toes. In this phase, as soon as you leave the ground, you start to bring the arms and legs into the required positions. When they are employed correctly, the arms help to provide enough impetus to reach the necessary height. In the lift phase, make sure that both your head and your upper body are tight. It is important to keep this tension to ensure that you jump vertically and do not change "direction."

▶ 3. Execution

This is the phase in which the jump itself is performed. Every jump is different, but each one is defined precisely. The main thing is that the arms and legs are brought into the correct positions for the jump in question.

Both arms and legs, and also the ball of the foot should be tensed to make a successful jump. In most cases, the feet remain pointed, but there are some jumps in which the foot can be flexed throughout.

Your face should not look tense or uptight. The difficulty of a jump should not show in the cheerleader's face; she should always smile naturally.

▶ **4. Landing**

When you come out of the jump and start to land, you should bring your legs and feet together as soon as possible, as landings are always two-footed. The feet should be parallel and the knees bent. A straight-legged landing stops your body from absorbing your body weight. Both feet should be as evenly loaded as possible.

Before you start jumping, you should always warm up and stretch thoroughly, as most jumps are enormously stressful for the muscles and joints.

6.3 DRILLS FOR JUMPING STRENGTH

Good jumping strength comes with practice. A simple but useful exercise is jumping in place. Jump with both feet together and try to jump higher every time. Repeat 10 times, and then do 10 more jumps only on the right foot and then 10 on the left foot. Always remember to bend your knees when you land.

An aerobic "step" is particularly suitable for the following exercise. If you don't have one available, you can use a sturdy box or just steps or stairs.

For this exercise, stand behind the step and jump in an even rhythm from the ground up onto the step. This exercise is particularly good for practicing the drop and the landing. The body develops a feeling for both phases and the joints are gradually prepared for the stress of complicated jumps.

6.4 DRILLS FOR UPRIGHT BODY POSITION WHEN JUMPING

In many jumps, an upright body posture is of fundamental importance, as in the kickline (see photo). The drills you can practice to learn a kickline help to develop an upright posture.

In a kickline, the legs are extended into the air and raised toward the chest; the foot is pointed. Many cheerleaders initially tend to lean forward in an attempt to bring their leg higher, which is a mistake. The upper body must remain upright during the whole kickline. Ideally, you should practice in front of a mirror.

Stand with your feet together and your hands behind each other's backs, so as to encourage a straight back. Now, alternately kick the right, and then the left legs into the air. It is important that the leg is locked as soon as it has left the ground. Repeat about five times on each side.

Always remember that the chest should remain upright and not move down toward the leg, and always pull your shoulders back.

In the next step, try the whole thing with a small jump, i.e., go into the prep together and bend the knees slightly, then raise your leg straight. The prep starts on a command from the coach on the count of 1; on the count of 2, the right leg is raised; on 3, you prep again; and on 4, the left leg is raised. You can repeat this as often as desired.

In cheerleading, we count from one to eight, which is addressed in the next chapter.

When you have mastered this exercise, make it a bit more difficult for yourself by putting several people in a row and have them do the same thing. The people standing in a row put their arms around each other's shoulders, so that the arms are stretched out to the left and right. The people stand next to each other and face forward (to a mirror or to the crowd). A kickline is especially popular in pre-game shows.

6.5 DRILLS FOR ARM AND LEG POSITION WHEN JUMPING

As mentioned above, the arms and the motions are very important in jumps, you should always be able to see your arms clearly and adjust their position in front of a mirror. You should learn the mirror image by heart and internalize it, as you don't have much time during the jump itself to think about where your arms should be. You can do the same thing for your legs. First, bring the right leg into the correct position for the jump, while you stand on the left leg normally and then vice versa.

Another drill for a good jump is a pair-work drill.

One team member stands behind a jumping cheerleader and supports her jump by holding her hips and deliberately pushing her upward during the take-off phase. She will obviously jump higher and get a sense of achievement. This drill can also be used for the toe-touch.

There are two ways of learning a jump:

1. Break the jump down into its component parts, learn these one after the other and only then perform them all together.
2. Perform the entire jump immediately and improve any mistakes gradually by repetition.

6.6 TYPICAL CHEERLEADER JUMPS AND THEIR CHARACTERISTICS

▶ **Tuck**

In this crouch jump, the upper body remains upright and the legs are tucked up toward the upper body, with bent knees. Make sure that the feet are together. Take off from and land on both feet. The arm position can be changed and means that the arms can be held in either the High V or the Touchdown positions.

▶ **Spread Eagle**
After taking off, extend the legs out to the side.

The knees face forward during the entire flight phase. It is very important that the upper body remains upright and that the hips do not bend. They should form a straight line with the upper body. In this jump, you take off from and land on both feet simultaneously. The arms are held in the Touchdown position.

▶ **Herkie**

This jump is named for the Lawrence Herkimer who was very influential in the development of cheerleading in the USA.

In this jump, one leg is extended out to the side at 90° and one leg is bent. The upper body is upright. The knee of the bent leg faces the ground and the other knee faces upward. This jump is not easy to learn.

In this jump, too, you take off from and land on both feet. One arm is in the Touchdown position and the other is on the hips.

▶ Toe Touch

The Toe Touch is one of the most popular and most-performed cheerleader jumps.

This jump is used in both cheers and in dances, and is particularly impressive for spectators. When you come out of the transition, you may feel like you want to touch your toes with your hands, but you shouldn't do it. In the toe touch, the cheerleader extends her legs to the side immediately after take-off, and tilts her hips forward. The legs should be brought up as high as possible, making sure that the knees face upward and not forward. As mentioned above, the cheerleader doesn't try to touch her toes, but to bring her arms up to the height of the arch of the foot. Trying to touch your toes stops you achieving the full hyper-extension necessary for this jump.

The arms are in the T position in this jump, and you take off from and land on both feet together.

▶ **Split**

This jump is essentially a split performed in the air. One leg should be held straight in front and one straight behind you. Both knees should be turned outward. The upper body is upright. The arms should be used to counterbalance the legs.

If the right leg is stretched forward, extend the left arm out to the side to balance it. The other arm can be placed on the hip or extended out to the right. Do not take off from both feet together for this jump, step right, left, right and then make a long stride with the left foot, which serves as a prep. This means that you take off from the left foot when the right leg is forward in the split. The right foot is then in front of the left for the landing.

▶ Double Nine

This jump is so-called because you must try to form two 9s with your arms and legs. It is one of the most difficult jumps in cheerleading.

In the jump phase, one leg is locked and pulled upward and at the same time the other one is bent so that the knee faces outward. The toes of the bent leg touch the knee of the straight leg, thus forming a 9. The arms should now be parallel to the legs. So, if the right leg is stretched out to the front, then the right arm should also be straight. Stretch the right arm above the right leg, with the hand forming a fist. The left arm is bent so that the fist touches the inside of the right arm near the elbow, thus forming the second 9.

The main thing to remember is that in the take-off, you bring the legs up to the arms, and not vice-versa, which would cause a lack of height. The head should not disappear between the arms, it should be held up.

In this jump, both feet are together for take-off and landing.

▶ Pike

In the Pike, the legs should be parallel to the ground. Immediately after take-off, the legs are raised and straight. At the same time, bend your chest toward your legs. Straighten the arms and touch your toes with your hands. Don't deliberately try to touch the toes, as this can prevent you from jumping as high as possible. In the Pike, both feet are together for take-off and landing.

6.7   DANCE JUMPS

Jumps are also used in dances, but they are not usually typical cheerleader jumps. However, they are easy to learn and put into practice.

▶ **Example 1**

In this jump, the knees are bent so that there is a 90° angle between the thighs and lower legs. Straighten the back leg so that the toes point upward and the knee faces downward, while the front leg is positioned so that the toes point downward. The arms are in a High V during this jump. Take-off and landing are both two-footed.

▶ Example 2

This jump is different from the others, as take-off and landing are both one-footed. If you bend the right leg, for example, then you take off from and land on the left leg.

The run up, or the prep, for this jump is as for the split, there is a double step (right, left, right), starting with the right leg, then take a long step with the left leg and take off from the left leg. For the lift, make sure you jump vertically and not horizontally. Both feet must definitely be pointed in this jump. The knee of the bent right leg points to the left and the back is straight and leaning slightly forward. The arms are in the High V position.

▶ Example 3

For this jump, use the same run up (prep) as for Example 2. It is different than the previous jump in that both legs are in the tuck position, with the knees at different heights. The take-off leg is placed slightly lower than the other leg. You also land on the take-off leg and the arms are also in the High V position.

The arm positions shown in these jumps may be varied; these are just the most commonly used motions.

7 DANCE

7.1 DANCE STYLES

This chapter is about dance. Dance has become the most important component of cheerleading for many teams. These teams are called dance teams.

If we look at the professional cheerleaders in the USA, we notice that they are nearly all dance teams. Following their example, the cheerleaders of the Professional NFL Europe League are also dance teams.

Although it may sound like dance teams only use dance moves, they actually include other cheerleader components like chants and motions.

The basic elements in the chapter on motions are fundamentally important, regardless of the team's chosen emphasis.

There are many ways of presenting the team in dances. The music, the formation, materials, costumes, pompoms, etc., all contribute to a good performance. All of this will be addressed later.

There are various dance styles, just as there are different teams, but the most commonly used dance styles are the following:

▶ Jazz

▶ Hip-Hop

▶ Funk

▶ Novelty

▶ Character

Which style is used for a dance depends in most cases on the music. The steps should always agree with the music, the speed, the text, the cuts in the music and the musical effects.

In dance, it is important that the team doesn't just dance, but actually presents something. This means that the team must know exactly how a dance works. Every cheerleader must know and master every single step. The team must be synchronized when they dance, must be able to transform themselves (be able to enter into a role) and to entrance the crowd.

Every dance should be different, in order to present a large repertoire of varied dance styles, but there are certain features that are valid for all dances.

Some dances are choreographed for a show to a certain piece of music, i.e,. a certain dance only goes with the music chosen for it. These dances are performed during the official game intervals, at the start and finish of a game, in the pre-game show, at halftime or in shows. There are also dances that are not choreographed for specific music. These dances are usually shorter and have no particular beginning or end. They are danced to any music during the game. These short dances are called Fillers or Eight Counts.

7.2   MUSIC

A dance is particularly effective if it has been well designed. The length of the dance is very important. A dance that is integrated into a show should be between 1 –1:50 minutes long. There are dances that last about 3:50 minutes though. You should make sure that long dances are not boring for the spectators. This can often happen with long dances because the music is frequently repeated. It is better to perform two short dances to different music than one long dance. Changes in musical genre and in dance style make the show more interesting.

The start and finish of a dance are crucial in making a real event out of a dance.

The start and finish of a dance should always convey something impressive and effective. Music can be very helpful as a signal that something is about to happen and as a way of directing the crowd's attention to the dance team.

In cheerleading, we separate music into counts. The smallest unit in a piece of music is the beat. A fast piece of music has a lot of beats per minute (bpm).

Eight beats form a phrase and, in cheerleading, we count everything in phrases, in groups of eight.

A movement can be executed on every count, for example, on 1,2,3,4,5,6,7,8 or on 1 and 2 and 3 and...

There are no real guidelines as to how many bpm a piece of cheerleading music should have. A fast song has about 125-160 bpm and a slow song can have 100-130 bpm.

The end of a song can also be well produced with the aid of music and effects.

But, in the beginning, the dance has to be learned. To do this, first listen to the music and especially the counts. When you listen to the beats, you know how fast a dance is. In a dance, there is a movement on every beat. Proceed in the same way as you did with cheers and chants. First, listen to and count with the music, then deal with the first 4-5 movements. Learn these movements (mostly by imitating the coach). Next, try to perform them in time with the music. When you have mastered this, move on to the next 4-5 movements. When you can perform the second part in time with the music, then perform it together with the first part and learn the third part. Continue like this until you have learned the whole dance.

Even in practice, you should make sure that you count the counts and beats in your head and not out loud, so that other people do not know that you are counting.

Another tip: While you are performing a step, you should already be thinking about the next step, so that none are forgotten and you don't lose the rhythm.

7.3 PROPS

Props are the aids and equipment used during a dance, and anything goes! You can use hats, sticks, chairs, scarves or fancy dress.

Like all cheerleaders, most dance teams work with pompoms (**see photo below**). Pompoms are the characteristic tools of the cheerleader. They come in all colors and many different materials. In a few dances, it is better to forget the pompoms and to use other kinds of props.

If you decide to dance with props, you must ensure that all participating cheerleaders can handle pompons. Performing with pompons is a great challenge. Even in practice, you must use props, otherwise mistakes creep into the routine.

Dance practice must always be carried out at 100%. Movements and step combinations should not be indicated, for in dance, many things must be mastered at the same time: personality, tightness of movements, body tension, formation changes, use of props, head position, etc., which can only be learned by practicing them frequently and in a professional manner.

7.4   FORMATION CHANGES

A dance is not just brought to life by unusual step combinations, jumps and props. Even perfect personality and execution are not enough to make a dance successful. Well-executed **formation change** by all cheerleaders is another important element. The change in positions brings movement to the whole group; the whole group dances and moves at the same time, not just individual dancers.

Formation changes show a completely different perspective and make the show livelier.

Many different scenarios may be presented at little cost and with simple resources.

In a formation change, it is important that everyone know exactly what she has to do. Every cheerleader must know her positions and how to get there. It is important that the participants don't get in each other's way and spoil the routine. Some cheerleaders walk, dance and move backward, others forward and some even sideways. You don't always move in your line of sight, so it is especially important that each girl knows and masters her exact path. This prevents collisions and embarrassing mistakes and makes what you do look good.

Formation change also makes it possible to make the best use of the available space. You should always try to use the breadth, depth and height of the space.

A group consisting of 10 cheerleaders can use the following formations:

▶ **Two Rows:**

. . . . .
. . . . .

▶ **Three Rows:**

. . .
. . . .
. . .

▶ **Pyramid: (no stunt)**

. . . .
. . .
. . .
.

The apex is at the front

▶ **Pyramid: (no stunt)**

The apex is at the back

▶ **A Row:**

▶ **Three Groups:**

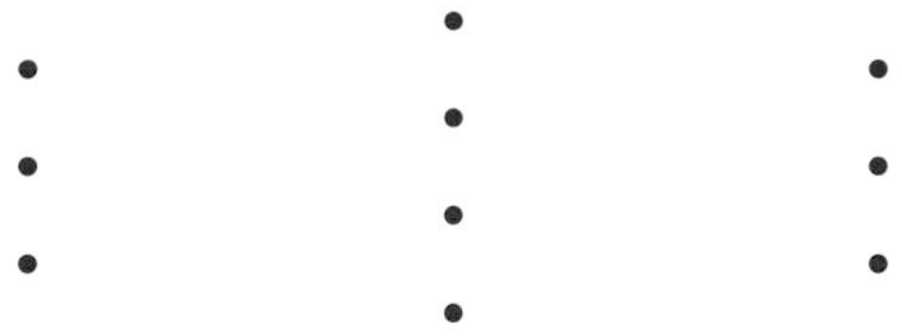

▶ **Three Groups:**

▶ **V-Formation:**

To the front

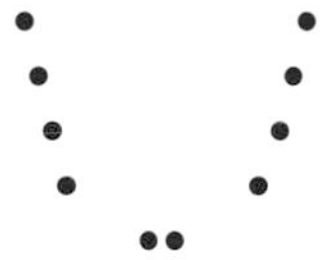

▶ **V-Formation:**

To the rear

▶ **Four Groups:**

Once the combination of steps, feeling for the rhythm of the music, use of the body, tension, props and formation change have been mastered, the dance team is ready to put their ability to the test in front of the public.

7.5   EXAMPLES

A filler is a short dance that can be danced to any music:

▶ **Count 1,2,3,4**
On the first four counts, take four steps forward, starting on the right foot.

At the same time, bring the arms up straight. First, hit a Low V, then a T-Motion, then a High V and lastly Jazz hands.

1

2

3

4

▶ **Count 5**

Jump back onto the right foot and extend the left leg in front of you. The arms are pushed forward at shoulder height. They are parallel and the hands form fists. The palms of the hands face downward.

▶ **Count 6**

On Count 6, jump so that both feet come together, and then hit a Half-T with the arms.

▶ **Count 7**
Jump with the legs apart, with the knees slightly bent and pointing outward like the toes. The arms are in the T-motion position.

▶ **Count 8**
On Count 8, jump and bring the feet together again, bring the arms into the sides of the body.

▶ **Count 1**

Start a Pivot Turn. This takes up four counts. On the first count, step forward with the right foot and hit a Low V with the arms.

▶ **Count 2**

Turn around to the rear, while the legs stay in the same place. The arms are brought into a Half-T, while you face backward.

▶ **Count 3**

On count 3, take a big step forward with the right foot and place it in front of the left foot. The arms are brought into the High V. You are still facing backward.

▶ **Count 4**

Now turn forward by bringing the left foot next to the right foot. The feet are parallel to each other and you face forward again. The arms are brought into the sides and touch the body.

▶ **Count 5**

Take a step to the right with the right foot, keeping the legs straight. Meanwhile, bring the left arm into the Half-T position. Extend the right arm downward and backward.

▶ **Count 6**

Change the above position and perform it on the left side this time, starting with a step to the left with the left foot.

▶ **Count 7**

Repeat the position from Count 5.

▶ **Count "and"**

The position remains largely the same, but the upper body now contracts and the back is now rounded.

▶ **Count 8**

Now relax again and take up the same position as in Count 7.

▶ **Count 1**

Jump with the legs apart, with the knees and toes pointing outward. The arms are in the T position.

▶ **Count 2**

On the second count, jump bringing the feet together with the legs slightly bent. The arms are in the Half-T position.

▶ **Count 3**
See count 1.

▶ **Count 4**
Bring the right leg into the pasé and straighten the left leg. The right arm is in the Touchdown position and the left hand is placed on the left hip. The body turns slightly to the side.

▶ Count 5

Bring the right arm downward over the head past the left ear. Step back onto the left foot. Place the left hand on the left hip.

▶ Count 6

Shift your weight onto your right foot, put the left foot forward and rest the toe of the pointed left foot on the ground. Bend the head backward and hold the left hand over the face. The right arm is at the side of the body and the upper body is hyper-extended backward.

▶ **Count 7**

Bring the upper body upright again and hit a Half-T position with the arms. Shift your body weight onto the left leg and bring your head forward again.

▶ **Count 8**

Take the right leg out to the right, and straighten both legs and bring the arms into the T-position. Lean forward.

▶ Count 1

Take a small step to the right with the right foot and touch the ground with the right toe, while stretching the arms up to the left holding them parallel to each other, looking in the direction of the arm movement.

▶ Count 2

Bring the arms down from top left to bottom right, while shifting the body weight onto the right foot. Point the left foot and place it on the ground. Bend both legs and look in the direction of the arm movement.

▶ **Count 3, 4**

Repeat movements from Counts 1 and 2 on the next two counts, but on the other side.

▶ **Count 5**

On the next four counts, take four steps backward starting on the right foot. Raise the arms above the head so that the palms of the hands touch each other.

▶ **Count 6**

On Count 6, step backward onto the left foot. Raise the arms behind the head.

▶ **Count 7**

Step back onto the right foot again. Push the arms backward in a Low V.

▶ **Count 8**

Step back onto the left foot, while crossing the arms in front of the chest.

After this count, start back at the beginning again, repeat as often as desired.

Please note that dances do not necessarily need to include cheerleader motions. There are also many dances that show another influence and are still highly suitable for a dance team.

8 STUNTS

8.1 PARTNER STUNTS AND PYRAMIDS

This chapter will describe what **partner stunts** and **pyramids** are and how to learn and form them.

Nearly every cheer team uses partner stunts or pyramids at some time. Many teams also work with both. A stunt is particularly impressive when it works well! It can be included in a cheer or presented to music during a break in the game.

Stunts include the formation of pyramids of various sizes with at least two people. We distinguish between double stunts, partner stunts and pyramids. Double stunts are usually carried out by two people, partner stunts by 3-4 people and pyramids by as many people as desired. These numbers do not include spotters, of course, who must always be present at any kind of stunt.

Pyramids are basically partner stunts, except that a pyramid is composed of several partner stunts performed next to each other or on top of each other.

8.2 STUNT ROLES

In every stunt, there are three different roles:

1. Base

2. Mounter

3. Spotter

1) The Base
The base is the person who remains on the ground in a stunt. She supports another cheerleader (the mounter) on her hands, shoulders, back, arms or legs. In pyramids, it is possible for the same cheerleader to be both a base and a mounter. This is the case when she is supported by a base and also supports someone else herself.

In other stunts, the base must always have contact with the ground. It is particularly important that her feet are square on the ground and she keeps good balance. She should always stand on the whole foot and not just on the toes. She looks forward, to the crowd, and watches the mounter form the stunt. It is equally important to watch the mounter on the dismount. The base must also ensure that the mounter lands back on the ground safely.

2) The Mounter

The mounter is the person who does not have ground contact during the stunt, as she is standing on one or more other people. The mounter requires very good basic body tension. The mounter must always maintain her posture and control herself. If she loses control just once during a stunt, the whole thing can collapse very quickly. A base may often have to help the mounter regain balance. Mounters are usually small, light and flexible.

3) The Spotter

A stunt should never be practiced without a spotter. The spotter is an additional person who supervises the whole proceedings but does not take part in the stunt. The spotter always stands where the mounter could fall, and, when necessary, intervenes and catches the mounter. In championships, the spotter should have absolutely no contact with the stunters. If he does intervene, the team has points deducted. A spotter should always be present when a stunt is being rehearsed. In practice, the spotter is also initially allowed to help during stunts. Even when the stunt is perfect, the spotter should be there, usually standing behind the stunt and only intervening if he sees that the mounter is about to fall.

8.3   STUNT SET UPS AND DISMOUNT

Every stunt consists of three phases:

1.   set up
2.   Execution
3.   Dismount

Each phase requires enormous concentration from all participants. Concentration, communication and, above all, timing are very important when learning stunts. The coach should always ensure that when she is explaining a stunt, there is a low level of noise in the sports hall. Quiet is important because everyone should know the stunt inside out before attempting it and because the coach is then able to explain the dangers of a stunt. She can also be sure that each of her instructions has been understood. Also, when it is noisy, you cannot hear your partner if she is in danger.

For situations like this, it is a good idea to agree on a special word that everyone will recognize as meaning that the cheerleader is in danger. For example, there may be times when the base can no longer support the mounter, and this word would let others know that the situation is serious without wasting time by using too many words.

Such a word could be "Careful" or "Down." If problems or difficulties arise in a particular phase, someone can shout "Down," the stunt is stopped and no one gets hurt. But before starting a stunt, each participant should know what she has to do. It has been proven that it is helpful not only to explain the stunt, but also to demonstrate it, for example in photos. Visualizing the stunt helps the cheerleaders to understand what it should look like.

Next, divide up the squad into smaller groups so that each group has at least one spotter and begin with the easiest stunt.

Go from easiest to hardest and learn the stunts one after the other.

Cheerleaders should stretch well before practicing stunts.

The following photos describe the phases and show what the stunts should look like.

It is also important to know the set up and dismount for each stunt thoroughly.

8.4   STUNTS (EXAMPLES)

a)   Doublestunts

▶ **Rear Tigh Stand**

Base:
The base places her legs wide apart in order to form a stable base, the knees and toes point outward. The hands are placed on the thighs above the bent knees to support the upright upper body, the head is held up.

Mounter:
The mounter stands behind the base. She places her hands on the base's shoulders and puts one leg on the base's hip flexor. She stands on this leg and pulls up the other leg. The second leg is positioned on the base's other hip flexor. It is important that the mounter stands on the very top of the base's legs, not on her thighs. Once the mounter is standing on both legs and can keep her balance, the arms are brought in the desired position, in this case, the High V.

▶ **Star**

Base:
The base makes a deep lunge forward. The front leg is bent and the rear leg is straight. The upper body is upright and the hands are placed on the hips, so that the fingers point downward. The elbows point backward.

Mounter:
The mounter stands behind the base and takes a 2 or 3 stride run up to gain momentum for the jump. The mounter takes off from both feet together, and supports herself with her hands on the base's shoulders. After the take-off, the legs are brought up and the mounter jumps onto the base's upper arms, without pushing her over. The legs are straight and the feet pointed.

▶ **Anchor**

Base:
The base stands with the feet slightly apart, to give better balance. The arms are stretched upward. It is important to maintain this stretch as the arms support the entire body weight of the mounter.

Mounter:
The base supports the mounter under her armpits. The mounter grips the inside of her legs and holds them far apart. The feet are pointed.

Set up:
The base goes into a crouch position in front of the mounter and holds the mounter under the armpits. On a command (one, two, down up), the mounter takes off from both feet as the base stands up. While the base is standing up, the mounter separates her legs and holds her knees. The base's arms should not bend at any time.

You can also go into this position from the Shoulder Sit, which is explained later.

▶ Lean-Back Stand

Base:

The base stands with her feet slightly apart and grips the mounter's left hand with her right hand. As soon as the mounter stands on the base's thighs, the base leans backward and grips the mounter's right knee with her left hand to stabilize her, while bending her legs slightly.

Mounter:

The mounter stands opposite the base. She gives her left hand to the base and stands with her left foot on the base's thigh. On a command, the mounter raises her right foot and positions it on the base's other thigh. At this point, the base and mounter lean backward, to give more stability. The mounter takes the right arm into the desired final position.

▶ Shoulder Sit

Base:
The base makes a lunge to the right, the knee and the toes also point to the right and her upper body leans forward. The base grips the mounter's right knee with her right hand and holds the mounter's foot with her left hand.

Mounter:
The mounter stands behind the base. She supports herself with her hands on the base's shoulders, then raises her right leg and puts her foot on the hip flexor of the base's thigh. On a command, the mounter takes off from the left foot and swings her left leg around the base's left shoulder. The base's right leg supports the weight.

Set up

▶ Shoulder Sit

Base:
Once the mounter has swung her left leg around the base's left shoulder, then the base grips this leg and holds it in place. The base now stands with the legs shoulder-width apart for better balance.

Mounter:
After swinging her left leg around the base's shoulder, the mounter distributes her body weight equally over both legs. Her upper body is upright and the arms can then be brought into the desired position.

▶ Shoulder Stand

Base:
The base takes up the same basic position as for the Shoulder Sit, except that the arms are not bent. They are held backwards so that the mounter can grip them. It is important that the elbows face forward, and the base also pulls the mounter's arms forward.

Mounter:
The mounter stands behind the base. Her right leg is put in the same position as for the Shoulder Sit. The mounter extends her arms forward to the base.

Set up I

Set up II

Base:
The base stands as before, but supports the mounter with her arms. The arms are raised and locked.

Mounter:
On a command, the mounter pushes off the ground from the left foot, with the help of the base's arms to support her. She places her left foot on the base's left shoulder, then raises her right foot and puts it on the base's right shoulder. The mounter straightens up and lets go of the base's hands.

▶ **Shoulder Stand**

Base:
The base stands up straight with her legs shoulder-width apart. By pushing the mounter's calves from behind she steadies her.

Mounter:
The mounter now stands upright on the base's shoulders, with her toes pointing forward and her arms brought into the desired position.

You can add the following element at the sides to liven up a pyramid or a partner stunt.

▶ **Leg Extension**

One person raises and straightens one leg and holds it firmly with her hand, making sure that both legs are completely straight and that her upper body remains upright.

She reaches her other hand out to the other person, who kneels to her right, with the toe of her front leg always placed out in front. This leg points toward the other person, but the upper body faces forward. The foot is pointed and only the toe touches the ground. One hand is placed on the hip, the other arm is linked with the other person's arm; both arms should be straight.

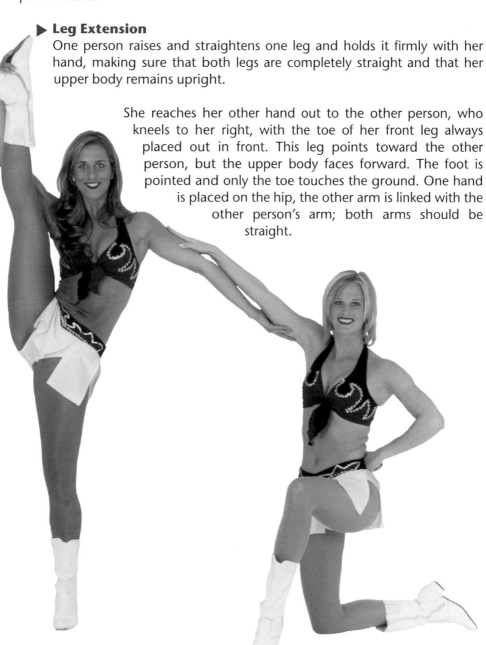

b) Partner Stunts

▶ Low Stand

Bases:
Both bases lunge toward each other, so that for both, the inside leg is bent and the outside leg is straight, and they both place their outside hand arm on their outside hips. The left base (looking from the crowd) grips the mounter's right knee and the other base prepares to hold the mounter's left leg.

The bases' inside feet should be parallel to each other, so that the right base's toes are level with the left base's heel and vice versa.

Mounter:
The mounter stands in between the two bases and, supporting herself with her hands on their inside shoulders, she puts her right foot on the inside thigh of the left base (as seen from the front).

Set up

▶ Low Stand

Bases:
The bases grip the mounter's ankles with their inside hand to support her. They are still in a lunge position and their backs are straight and they lean forward. Their outside arms can now be brought into the desired position.

Mounter:
The mounter has pulled up her left leg and placed it on the thigh of the other base. She stands up, extending her legs and upper body. Hit a High V.

Bases:

The bases hold the mounter's hand with their outside hands and watch the mounter's movements. They let go of her ankles.

Mounter:

The mounter grips the bases' outside hands, holds her arms straight out to the sides and prepares to jump. On a command, she jumps off the bases' legs and lands on both feet together.

Dismount I

Bases:
On a command, the mounter jumps off the bases' thighs, while the bases hold under the mounter's armpits with their inside hands to stop her swinging. They are responsible for the mounter's landing safely.

Mounter:
The mounter's arms are locked throughout to make it easier for the bases to stop her.

She lands with both feet together.

Dismount II

▶ **Double Base Shoulder Stand**

Bases:
The bases take up the same positions as for the Low Stand, except that the mounter holds the bases' upstretched outside arms. The left base (seen from the front), holds the mounter's right knee, thus stabilizing her. The right base holds the mounter's ankle, which is placed on her right shoulder.

The third base stands behind the mounter and steadies her. She should support and intervene, as this is a practice situation and not a competition.

Mounter:
The mounter holds the two bases' outside hands to support herself. On a command, she takes off from her left foot and places it on the right base's right shoulder. On a second command, she pulls up her left leg and places it on the left base's left shoulder.

The second command is also a signal for the bases to come out of the lunge.

Set up

Double Base Shoulder Stand

Bases:
The bases now stand with both legs straight and lean forward, with their outside hands on their hips and with their inside hands steadying the mounter.

Mounter:
The mounter's body weight is distributed evenly over both legs. Her whole body is extended and her hands are on her hips.

The third base steadies the mounter by holding the back of her calves.

Bases:
Both the bases hold the mounter's outside hands with their outside hands and prepare for the jump, which is exactly the same as the Low Stand.

Mounter:
The mounter holds the bases' hands and on a command, jumps off their shoulders.

Both she and the bases bend their knees throughout the landing, never land with straight legs. They are only straightened after the landing.

Dismount

▶ **Double Base Elevator**

Although this stunt looks similar to the Double Base Shoulder Stand, it is actually different.

Bases:

The bases stand opposite each other, the legs are shoulder-width apart and the knees slightly bent. The upper body should be kept upright. The hands are held in front of the body, so that the mounter can put her foot inside. The fingers point into the centre, the palms of the hands upward. The thumbs must point outward.

Mounter:

The mounter supports herself on the bases' shoulders nearest to her and places her right foot in the hand of the left base.

Set up I

Bases:
The right base catches the mounter's right foot. Otherwise, the bases remain in the same position as before.

Mounter:
On a command, the mounter lifts her right foot from the ground. The left base catches it in the air. The mounter is in a crouch position, with her feet in the hands of the bases. She supports herself on the bases' shoulders.

Set up II

▶ Double Base Elevator

Bases:
Once the second base has gripped the mounter's other foot, the bases stand up and straighten their legs, holding the mounter in their hands. The mounter's feet should be at shoulder height. The bases' front hand grips the toes and the back hand the heels.

Mounter:
The mounter stands up as soon as the second base has taken hold of her foot. It is important that the bases hold the mounter's feet at the same height so that she can stand up straight away. The whole body must be under tension. The arms are then placed in the desired position.

Variation
If the mounter feels secure, you can perform the following variation.

Bases:

The bases raise their front hand up to the mounter. This can only work if the mounter transfers her weight onto her heels so that the bases can remove their front hands from the mounter's feet. The bases watch the mounter and prepare for the dismount.

Mounter:

The mounter transfers her body weight backwards slightly, onto her heels. She then grips the bases' hands and on a command, jumps down from the bases' rear hands.

Dismount I

Bases:
The bases raise their rear hands to catch and stop the mounter as she falls.

Mounter:
The mounter dismounts and keeps her arms locked to make it easier for the bases to catch them. The mounter bends her knees as she lands.

Dismount II

▶ **Russian Split**

Bases:
Three bases are required for this partner stunt, and they all start off in a crouch position. The base on the left (as seen from the crowd) holds the mounter's ankle with her right hand and her thigh with her left hand. The center base puts both hands under the mounter's bottom. The bases' fingers point inward. The right base holds the mounter's other ankle with her left hand and places her right hand under the mounter's other thigh. The right bases' fingers point away from her. They must release and turn their hands on the upward movement, so that they can stabilize the mounter in the end position.

The left base's hands are already in the correct position, as they are holding the right leg, which is raised in the air.

As the mounter takes off from the ground on a command, the bases stand up and lift the mounter into the air. The bases extend both their arms and legs.

Mounter:
The mounter stands between two bases and in front of another base. She extends her right leg out to the right. Her upper body is kept upright and she supports herself with her hands on the shoulders of the bases to her right and left.

Set up

▶ **Russian Split**

Bases:
The bases stand in a small semi-circle with their legs straight and shoulder-width apart. Their arms are upstretched and they support the mounter with their hands. The center base's hands are both underneath the mounter's bottom. The other two bases both support the mounter's ankle and thigh.

Mounter:
The mounter sits on the bases' hands. Her legs are stretched out to the sides and her upper body is upright. Her arms are held in a High V.

Bases:

The two outside bases come together to stand facing each other for the dismount, bringing the mounter's straightened legs together as they do so. The center base stays where she is and does not move.

Mounter:

The mounter brings her arms from a High V into a Low V. Her upper body remains upright, and she allows the bases to bring her legs into another position. The mounter must now keep her balance.

Dismount I

Bases:

The bases bend their arms and let the mounter's feet touch the ground first, without letting her go. Their hands still hold the mounter until her feet reach the height of their hips, and only then do the outside bases let go. They release their outside hands and support the torso. The center base supports the main body weight and she too bends her arms and joins in the downward movement. The mounter is thus brought safely to the ground.

Dismount II

▶ Split

Bases:
The bases crouch down next to each other, with their upper bodies both facing in the same direction. They raise their outside arm, which is then gripped by the mounter. Their arms must be kept tight. The right, rear, base holds the mounter's right ankle with her inside hand, with her thumb pointing downward and backward and the fingers pointing toward the other base.

Mounter:
The mounter stands between the two bases with her feet apart, with the left foot slightly forward. She holds her arms out straight to the sides and grips the bases' hands.

Set up I

Bases:
On a command the bases stand up and the mounter jumps off the ground.

With their inside hands, they pull the mounter's legs apart and lift them up. The arms are raised above the head during the whole upward movement.

Mounter:
On a command, the mounter takes off from the ground from both feet, at the same time separating her legs, as if she was going to do a split in the air. She holds the bases' hands to support herself, and keeps her arms locked.

Set up II

▶ Split

Bases:
The bases stand with their feet shoulder-width apart. They both turn to the side, and the rear base extends her right arm upward so that she can support the mounter. With her left hand she holds the mounter's right foot, which is positioned on her left shoulder.

The front base holds up her left arm, with which she also supports the mounter. With her right hand she holds the mounter's other foot, which is placed on her left shoulder.

A third base can also stand in the center and hold the mounter's legs.

Mounter:
The mounter does the splits on the bases' shoulders, stretching her arms out to the sides and supporting herself by holding the bases' hands.

c) Pyramids

No explanations are given for the photos below; they are just for inspiration. In the formation, always remember that a pyramid is built from the bottom up and just one step at a time. Don't forget that enough spotters should be on hand to intervene if necessary.

9 TUMBLING

Tumbling has become an important part of cheerleading in the past few years in Europe. Tumbling means nearly all the elements of floor gymnastics, from the forward roll, to the handstand to the somersault.

Many teams practice tumbling. A few have particularly good tumblers who can even shine at flic-flacs, etc. Well-executed elements are spectacular and particularly attractive for the spectator, but they are also difficult to learn.

It often takes years to learn certain elements. Don't try to master every element, as the risk of injury is very high in tumbling. Most teams proceed as follows: they learn elements that are not so difficult or dangerous to learn, e.g., a cartwheel or a handstand. These elements can be carried out by the whole team, with the right training.

Cartwheel

Handstand

In many teams, there are also members who used to be gymnasts. These cheerleaders can often perform such moves as the walkover (c.f. photo) or a flic-flac. It is therefore an advantage for the team to integrate a tumbling team into their cheerleading team. Those who belong to the tumbling team perform tumbling elements in certain situations, while the other cheerleaders do something different.

Walkover

It is now up to the coach to combine both groups well. If the program order is correctly planned, it can look very impressive.

Tumblers can be used while the team builds a pyramid, for example. It looks good when 2 or 3 cheerleaders perform tumbling routines in front of the pyramid.

Elements that are mastered by the whole team can also be incorporated into a dance or a cheer.

Like chants, tumbling segments can be used:

▶ **During the whole game**

▶ **At the start of the game**

▶ **When the players are running onto the field**

▶ **After a successful play**

▶ **In a cheer or a dance**

Before performing tumbling elements, you must be absolutely sure that you have mastered them.

To learn these elements, you should definitely turn to a gymnastics club, where there are trained coaches who specialize in acrobatics and can provide further assistance.

Tumbling should always be preceded by warm-up and stretching.

10 PERFORMANCE, RULES AND STYLING

To be a cheerleader, you need to be more than just a good dancer, jumper or tumbler, etc. A good cheerleader must learn, accept and practice certain aspects of the sport.

You must differentiate between the private individual and the person that you assume when you wear a cheerleading uniform. From the day you are given a uniform, you must know how to behave in public. For to be a cheerleader is not just a fun thing to do, it also brings with it responsibility.

a) Performance

The way in which a cheer squad enters an arena or a sports hall is very important, as this is when professionalism begins. It is important that the whole team is dressed the same when they enter. The uniform is the first thing that spectators notice. To show that you form a unit, the whole outfit should be the same, not just the costumes. Make sure that all members wear the same shoes, trousers and jackets. Synchronicity starts here.

Even the bags can be the same. If a team is completely new and does not yet have uniform clothes, then at least make sure that all the clothes are the same color. The same goes for the shoes. You can at least decide that everyone has white gym shoes and black jackets. From the start you should make an effort to achieve a harmonious appearance. Hair and make-up also play an important part. There will be more on this later.

There should always be one person within the group who sorts out organizational problems. This person has contact with the organizer, knows the contents of the contract and deals with the necessary details to organize an appearance and provide a good show. Things like who operates the music system, where the stage is, etc. Meanwhile, the other cheerleaders can relax; they are always nice and friendly. Friendliness is an important quality that every cheerleader should strive for. You should always have a natural smile on your lips for the guests present, don't force it! (**c.f. photos next page**).

Exaggerated

Too serious

Just right

You should also be open and approachable. It is quite OK to talk with guests or with the press, but always be careful what you say. In such conversations, you should not give away information about other cheerleaders, about the organization or about the team. Questions about private addresses, etc., should not be asked or answered, for in public, you should separate the private person from the cheerleader.

After the show, the team should leave together. They should travel back in the same clothes in which they arrived.

b) Rules

There are certain rules that many cheerleader teams already follow. These rules are there to protect the whole team; they should ensure that the cheerleader achieves a good, unified public image. While a cheerleader is wearing her uniform and representing the team in public, she should observe the following rules.

A cheerleader should:

▶ **Always be punctual at practice and at appearances**

▶ **Always practice her routines, jumps, cheers, etc., before practice**

▶ **Not miss a practice session without a good reason**

▶ **Not wear jewelry in practice or appearances**

▶ **Not wear brightly-colored nail polish**

▶ **Under no circumstances smoke or drink alcohol in public**

▶ **Not eat when wearing her costume**

▶ **Not have piercings on her face**

▶ **Stick to the dress code**

▶ **Trust her coach**

▶ **Always be ready to help her teammates**

▶ **Always consider the welfare, harmony and reputation of the team**

These rules protect the team and each individual cheerleader. Sticking to these rules can avoid many problems.

c) Styling

Hair and make-up naturally help to create a unified appearance, and they are part of the dress code along with clothing. (**photo – right**).

Every team decides for itself which hairstyle the members want to wear and how they want to make themselves up. The only important thing is that everyone in the team sticks to it. If the coach decides on a ponytail, then all the cheerleaders in the team should wear a ponytail. If she would prefer that all cheerleaders wear their hair loose, then no one should turn up with their hair in a ponytail. The same goes for make-up.

It is not necessary for all team members to wear the same make-up, as skin-type, face shape and eye color differ from one person to another, so it is difficult to find make-up that suits everyone. Deciding on a certain lipstick color and the intensity of the make-up can already go some way to ensuring a unified look. But these decisions are made by the team and the coaches. There are also teams whose cheerleaders wear identical make-up, which is also fine. The main thing is that everyone understands the decisions and that everyone is totally present. Presence shows as soon as you step onto the field or the stage.

There is nothing more to say about hair, it just rounds off the image.

d) Be a Role Model
Cheerleaders may take part in very diverse events and also do things that are not typical cheerleader functions. But it is all still cheerleading.

A cheerleader meets many different people at events and public appearances. In the crowd, there are children, young people, men and women.

Not everyone is familiar with the sport of cheerleading and for many, your performance will be their first experience of it. This makes it all the more important to make a good impression, for at that moment, you represent everyone who participates in the sport. Show that cheerleading is a legitimate sport and behave responsibly, for you are representing all cheerleader teams.

Cheerleaders should have good manners, not just a good appearance. You should enjoy your time as a cheerleader, as you will travel around a lot and learn much that will help you in later life. Be an example and role model for all the children and young girls who want to be cheerleaders one day. Show them how to behave and what it is all about.

Be proud of what you do, know, learn and experience, for it is something SPECIAL.

CHEERLEADING

SPECIAL THANKS TO

▶ The General Manager of the Rhein Fire Football team Company GmbH, Alexander Liebkind
▶ The Rhein Fire Cheerleader Team:
  In particular: Jasmin H. Svenja G., Petra S., Sandra M., Katja G., Miriam C., Kerstin L. and Margarethe S.
▶ Private Scholar Dr. Theo Stemper
▶ My husband, Jörn Lange
▶ My family
▶ The Rhein Fire office staff

And the photographers:

▶ Ralph Peters
▶ Ralf König
▶ Olaf Grendel
▶ Jürgen Leisman
▶ Katrin Kedziora
▶ Daniel Gregorz
▶ Marian Sell

PHOTO CREDITS

Cover layout: Jens Vogelsang

Photos (inside): Ralph Peters, Ralf König, Olaf Grendel, Jürgen Leisman, Katrin Kedziora, Daniel Gregorz & Marian Sell

Photos (cover): dpa Picture-Alliance

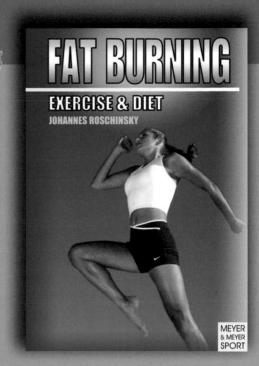

ISBN: 978-3-1-84126-140-9
$ 17.95 US
£ 12.95 / € 16,90

ISBN: 978-3-1-84126-243-7
$ 17.95 US
£ 14.95 / € 16,95

ISBN: 978-3-1-84126-025-9
$ 17.95 US
£ 12.95 / € 16,90

ISBN: 978-3-1-84126-021-1
$ 17.95 US
£ 12.95 / € 16,90

ISBN: 978-3-1-84126-175-1
$ 14.95 US
£ 9.95 / € 14,95

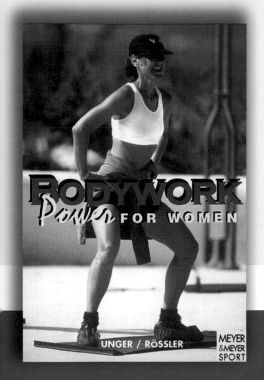

ISBN: 978-3-1-84126-022-8
$ 17.95 US
£ 12.95 / € 16,90

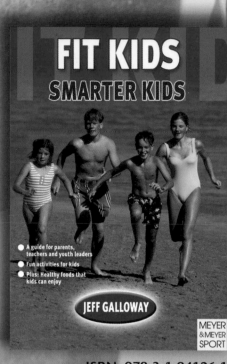
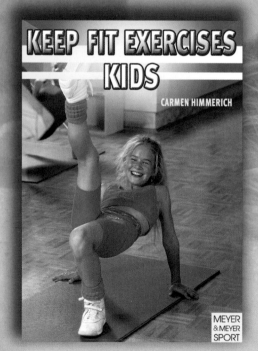

MEYER
&MEYER
SPORT

MEYER & MEYER Sport | www.m-m-sports.com